AF264333

Viable

THE TRUTH OF CHRIST'S LOVE

Viable

THE TRUTH OF CHRIST'S LOVE

ENDORSEMENTS FOR *Viable*

Viable is a heart-warming, triumphant story of a mother heavy-laden with secret shame, sorrow, and self-condemnation for 30 years because of her choice—until she experiences the healing, renewing, and restorative love of Jesus Christ in a most unexpected and unusual way. Here is what others have said about *Viable*:

"*Viable* handles a controversial and sensitive issue with grace."

**- Dr. Richard Gibbons, Senior Pastor,
First Presbyterian Church of Greenville, SC**

"*Viable* is a captivating and compelling story. It takes you on an emotional roller coaster that resolves into a beautiful story of love and forgiveness."

**- Carol Tobias, President of the
National Right to Life Committee**

"In a powerfully gripping way, *Viable* deals with regret and remorse felt by so many who have made the decision to terminate new life – even knowing instinctively that their choices were not founded upon truth. The story deals with anger, denial, indoctrination, confession, forgiveness, and healing. A must-read for those who want to see life as God does and for others who need healing from past decisions."

**- Carter Conlon, General Overseer,
Times Square Church, 51ˢᵗ & Broadway, New York City**

"*Viable* was very personal for me. It's also good for men and boys to understand that they play a very real part in the decision of a woman to terminate her pregnancy. I pray that healing will come to them all."

**- Kathy Forck, co-coordinator for the
Columbia, Missouri 40 Days for Life Campaign**

"I knew that *Viable* would be impactful and it was."

**- Dr. Joronda Crawford, Co-Founder of the
Pro-Life Pro-Family Coalition of Chicago**

"*Viable* graciously presents God's forgiveness and His desire to heal those who know abortion all too well. Keep your tissues handy!"

- Lori Rousch, Chapter Leader, Deeper Still Arkansas

"I learned from *Viable* that the truth, once told, can lead to forgiveness, a rebuilding of trust, and healing in relationships, whether they be between you and God or you and your family. Truth can be acutely painful and very difficult, but in the end the pain is a small price to pay."

**- Reverend Mr. Larry Hart,
St. Catherine of Siena Church, Orange Park, Florida**

"I feel a lot of girls should see *Viable* to get a better understanding of things because this is not what they are teaching us in school."

- 13-year-old reader

"*Viable* brings into a real-world environment the effect abortion has on women and families."

- United States Congressman Joe Wilson

"Wow. If *Viable* doesn't move you, nothing will."

- South Carolina Attorney General Alan Wilson

"*Viable* is about real life and how the decisions we make can change the way we look at our spouse, our family, our friends, and even our God. As you relate to the story, I'm certain that you will laugh, cry, and ultimately be encouraged and enlightened."

**- River Sussman, CEO of
Obria Medical Pacific Northwest**

"*Viable* is a must-read. In a refreshing way, it deeply resonates with men and women alike, regardless of their emotional fortitude. It delicately unfurls layers of complexity and presents a myriad of nuances that vividly illustrate the profound impact of abortion on our communities."

**- Esther Ripplinger, President & CEO,
Human Life of Washington**

"Creative, powerful, moving, thought-provoking, grace-centered, authentic, and soberingly presented are words that reflect my reaction to *Viable.* Most significantly, the power of the Gospel of Jesus Christ to bring about honesty, forgiveness, healing, and restoration is soundly declared."

**- Tim Reed, Pastor,
Covenant Presbyterian Church - Little Rock, AR**

"*Viable* is a story steeped in the Christian faith and a recognition that our God is a forgiving God who seeks reconciliation with His children regardless of their pasts."

**- Dave Andrusko,
National Right to Life Today**

"*Viable*: The potential to change the world."

- Support After Abortion

"*Viable* is Holy Spirit-inspired and will open your eyes to the long-term effects of abortion. I promise your heart will NEVER be the same!"

- Sylvia Blakely RN, MS, Founder of Arise Daughter and Arise Artists Post-Abortion Healing Ministries

"The story is incredibly compelling because abortion can affect everything in life [unless] you go to the Lord seeking the forgiveness and redemption of Jesus Christ. That message came through very clearly."

- Tony Beam, Palmetto Family Council Board Member and Senior Director of Church and Community Engagement and Public Affairs, North Greenville University

"*Viable* won me over from the start as it championed human life with bold Christian integrity and moving sensitivity!"

- Deborah Hollifield, Past Executive Director, Presbyterians Protecting Life

"These words are remarkable and the characters are superlative."

- South Carolina Governor Henry McMaster

DEDICATION

To Karen Iacovelli Forster,
who first brought *Viable* to the stage.

TABLE OF CONTENTS

PART ONE

---

*"In your anger do not sin: Do not let the sun go down while
you are still angry, and do not give the devil a foothold."*
Ephesians 4:26-27 (NIV)

The church nursery, housed in the basement, is dark and
shadowy. Several narrow basement windows set high on
the cinderblock wall are barely identifiable in the glow of
a nearby streetlight. Occasionally, the headlights of passing cars il-
luminate portions of the long room as they splash past the church
on the rain-soaked street outside. With each passing car, the light
coming through the raindrop-spotted basement windows falls on a
circle of empty and motionless old-fashioned wooden rocking chairs.

As each car moves closer to the church, the beams of the headlights
creep across the wall revealing large, colorful letters of the alphabet,
equally colorful numbers, cardboard posters of animals, including
lions, sheep, cows, pigs, camels, and fish – most notably a whale – as
well as baby cribs with wooden slat sides, and playpens enclosed by
nets. There are also momentary glimpses of a changing table with
colorful plastic shapes suspended above it, a doll house, rugs with

vegetable cartoon characters, as well as scenes featuring various biblical characters in first-century robes and head coverings surrounded by children in contemporary school clothes printed on the rugs. Toys fill a large, wooden toy box as several toy trucks, boats, and a doll lay on the floor nearby.

As the headlights of the last vehicle begin to fade away, the final glimpse illuminates a framed picture of Jesus with his flowing brown hair and brown eyes hanging on the wall beside the doorway to the nursery.

Suddenly, a pair of headlights approaches the basement window nearest the door, backlighting a steady and sizable rainfall. The headlights go out and the driver's side door opens. A woman wearing a skirt gets out of the car quickly, pulls the hood of her raincoat over her head, and slams the door shut. She enters through one of a pair of heavy wooden doors at the top of the basement stairs. The door creaks as she pulls it open and steps through, and it creaks again as it closes on its own. Pausing for a moment, the woman shakes the raindrops off of her coat onto the large welcome mat, points her car key chain toward the door, pushes a button, and listens until she hears a faint beep as her car locks.

The woman ascends another short flight of steps and hesitates at the top. "Hello?" she calls out tentatively.

There is no answer.

She looks back at the door and then turns to look down the long, dark hallway in front of her.

"Hello?" she calls out a second time, a bit louder, her voice echoing slightly against the hallway walls and tile floor along with the sound of her footsteps as she slowly and cautiously walks about thirty feet down the hall. It is illuminated only by a red EXIT sign above the doors she just entered through. A few remaining raindrops on her coat fall onto the floor and her chunky boots as she continues, holding her car keys in her right hand, her finger poised over the security alarm button. She runs her hand along the wall in hopes of encountering a light switch.

"George?" she calls out.

Still no answer.

She can hear the swish of cars passing the church building on the soaked pavement outside. A voice speaking at a conversational volume would be easily audible had there been one. The woman stops and, peering out from under her rain hood, looks back toward the door where she entered.

"Pastor Phil?" she calls out, turning back toward the hallway. Her echoing voice trails off into darkness and silence.

Suddenly, the glare of fluorescent light pours out of the open door of a room she is standing in front of. She gasps and twists her body abruptly toward the light, clutching her purse straps. She raises her left hand and sweeps the rain hood back off of her head. The silence is deafening. Moving ever so cautiously, she tilts her head to her right and peers into the room, then does the same thing tilting her head to the left.

The fifty-ish, professionally-dressed woman, wearing a wedding band on her left hand, stands in the door of the room for a moment, looking puzzled. Finally, she takes a deep breath, holds it in her lungs, and steps inside the door, still scanning the room from her improved vantage point.

"This isn't funny, George," she scolds as she crosses the threshold. The windowless room is empty. The room decor was contemporary forty years ago, but now shows wear from decades of use. The twelve chairs in the room, arranged in a circle, feature wooden frames with blue fabric cushioned seats and backs.

A three-cushion sofa with several throw pillows, its back to the door, occupies a portion of the circle. A single wing chair faces the sofa from the opposite side. Assorted books on shelves line each wall, arranged spine out, with an occasional stack of similarly spined books laying on their sides, suggesting classes meet here. Despite the room being carpeted, an oval-shaped throw rug covers the floor in the center of the seating circle.

After a moment, she turns, leans out, and peers back down the hallway toward the entrance doors. Seeing no one, she looks at her wrist watch, places the straps of her purse back on her shoulders, and slowly enters the room. Stepping away from the door slightly, she removes her cell phone from her purse and touches the screen several times.

"Call George," she instructs the phone.

Moments later, the creak of the big wooden doors under the EXIT sign is drowned out by the chirping of a cell phone announcing an incoming call. The woman timidly peeks out of the door.

"I'm right here," a man's voice announces, a tad bit of annoyance in his tone. The woman's shoulders drop as tension is released and a gushing exhale escapes her lips. As echoing footsteps climb the stairs and approach in the hallway, the woman hangs up the call and returns the cell phone to her purse along with her car keys. She removes her raincoat and hangs it on the iron coat rack beside the door. She wears a navy blue suit jacket over a white blouse and a matching navy blue skirt.

Just then, a six-foot-tall man about the woman's age with salt-and-pepper hair and wearing a raincoat enters the room as if he is in familiar territory. He wiggles his cell phone over his head to show he heard her incoming call. George slips his cell phone into the side pocket of his raincoat before wriggling out of it, revealing his business suit, wrinkled from the day. He wears a gold wedding band on his left hand. He hangs his raincoat on the iron coat rack and leans toward the woman to kiss her.

The woman turns away from him sharply and marches to the sofa, where she plops down in the corner with her back toward him. She sets her purse on the floor in front of her and arranges a couple of throw pillows behind her on the sofa.

George stands frozen for a moment, his lips still pursed for the kiss. He blinks his eyes a couple of times and sighs.

"I thought these sessions were supposed to start at six," the woman scolds as she settles back into her nest of pillows.

George straightens up and looks at his watch as he walks behind the sofa, pauses, and shows his wristwatch to the woman.

"That's what I have, Judy. Six o'clock. Straight up."

"I know," Judy acknowledges with a whine. "But we always used to get here five minutes early to settle." George sighs again, walks to the wing chair opposite the sofa, removes his suit coat, drapes it ceremoniously over the back of a wood-framed chair next to him, loosens his tie, unbuttons the top button of his white shirt, and gently sits down.

"There," he announces, "I'm settled." George looks at his watch again. "And I still have six o'clock."

Not amused, Judy rolls her eyes, then looks around the room. "Where's Pastor Phil?"

George looks around. "I don't know."

"It's not like him to be late."

George and Judy sit in silence for a few uncomfortable moments. They occasionally look at each other and then away. George finally pushes himself back to his feet, slides his hands into his pockets, walks over to a bookshelf, and begins inspecting the titles. Another few moments go by before he breaks the silence.

"This was always my least favorite part," he confesses without turning back toward his wife.

"Which part is that?"

"Waiting," George answers. "Waiting here. With you." He turns back toward the sofa to survey the damage. Judy looks up at George as if to say something but decides better of it and another long pause ensues as the two of them look at each other in a deflated, hopeless way.

"Do you think this silence was any easier for me?" Judy finally queries.

George blinks a couple of times and sighs. He turns back toward the bookshelf.

"I guess not," he admits. He pulls a book off the shelf, examines the cover front and back for a disinterested moment, slides it back in place, turns, and surveys the room. "This place always seemed so sterile. Modern church. Most everything is straight, rigid, and cold." George turns and looks at Judy. "The only soft and inviting things in here are the sofa and the wing chair."

Detecting the snarky accusation, Judy stares George down for a moment before she again decides not to engage and turns away, looking at her watch again. "I wonder where he is," she blurts out, more agitated than before.

"Maybe he's stuck in traffic," George offers.

"He always used to walk over from his office across the hall," she says as if the mere mention of it would make Pastor Phil appear.

"Everything was dark when I came in," George continues. "Not a light in the place except in here."

Judy stands up, walks to the door and stares into the dark hallway, looking one direction and then the other. George watches her as she walks across the hall, her footsteps echoing again. George hears her wiggling the knob on a door in the dark before she reappears in the doorway. "Well...?" he asks.

"Locked," Judy reports as she stands in the doorway, looking perplexed. "There isn't a light on anywhere. I'm amazed the front doors were unlocked. Are you sure that Pastor Phil wanted to see us tonight at six o'clock?"

"I didn't talk to Phil. I just came at six like you told me to."

"I didn't tell you to be here at six."

"Okay, you *texted* me to be here at six. What's the difference?"

"I didn't text you about coming tonight at all," Judy clarifies as she walks back to the sofa. "You texted *me*."

She sits defiantly.

"Slow down, honey," George cautions as he walks from the bookcase to the coat rack and retrieves his cell phone from the pocket of his raincoat. He walks back to the wing chair pressing buttons on the screen. Finding what he's looking for, he sits down, leans forward, and holds the screen out where she can see it. "I have it right here. 'Meet me at church. Six o'clock.' It's from your phone at three o'clock this afternoon."

Judy woman leans forward to get a closer look. Looking annoyed, she pulls her cell phone out of her purse and taps the screen a few times and holds it up for George to see. He leans in for a closer look.

"Session at church. Six o'clock," he reads aloud.

"It's from your cell phone," Judy says confidently. "At three o'clock."

"What the..? I never sent that," George insists.

"Well, I never sent the text you received."

"What do you make of that?" George asks inquisitively. "Did you talk to Phil?"

"I haven't spoken to the Pastor since the last time I came to church."

"Christmas Eve?" George asks incredulously. Judy nods her head.

"That was over a month ago," George exclaims. "Did he tell you *then* that he wanted to talk to us?"

"No. He just asked how we were doing."

George leans back in his chair and looks at Judy suspiciously. "What did you tell him?"

"I told him the standoff continues."

It's George's turn to roll his eyes. "Always my fault, of course."

"I didn't intimate whose fault it is," she defends.

"Well, that's probably what he wants to talk to us about." George slips his cell phone into his inside suit coat pocket.

Judy studies her phone again.

"Except…" she says.

"Except what?"

"Except that neither of us talked to him, and it doesn't appear that he texted anyone."

George ponders for a moment before slapping his thighs and standing up. "Well, that's that then," he says confidently as he reaches for his suit jacket. "All is not lost. I still have time to catch the game on TV."

"Where are you going?"

"Home."

"That's so like you," Judy says in a disgusted tone.

"Oh, here we go," George moans.

"Aren't you the least bit curious about what's going on?"

"Nope."

"George!" she exclaims as he walks to the coat rack and begins to don his raincoat.

"Forget it, Judy," he pleads, turning back to her. "Your cell phone has a text from me that I never sent. My cell phone has a text from *you* that you *say* you never sent. There's not a light on in the building, which makes me suspect that Pastor Phil never had any intention of talking to us tonight and is, at this moment, probably at home in front of his TV getting ready to watch the tip off."

"Be serious."

"I am serious. This is a fluke. It's all just a weird ending to a l-o-n-g day. See you at home."

George heads for the door.

"Do you remember why we came to this room in the first place, all those years ago?" Judy calls after him.

George pauses in the doorframe and his shoulders droop. He stands for a moment with his back to Judy.

"Is that why you tricked me into coming here tonight?"

Judy leaps to her feet, angrily wagging her index finger.

"I did not trick you into coming here any more than you tricked me," she shouts.

George turns slowly toward his wife.

"Then let's call it even and go home," he says evenly.

Obviously agitated, Judy folds her arms across her chest and turns her back on him.

"Maybe later."

George sighs and walks slowly toward Judy. He gently rests his hands on her shoulders. She stiffens. "Honey, this room doesn't conjure good memories for me. I'm not comfortable here."

Judy jerks her shoulders away from George's hands.

"I'm not comfortable at home," she barks.

George ponders her comment for a moment, walks back to his wing chair, and sits. "Look," he says softly. "We tried. Even Pastor Phil tried. We talked, we prayed..."

"And *you quit*," Judy blurts, pointing her finger at him.

George sits up straight in his chair.

"That's a 'You' statement," he parleys back, demonstrating that he has been in a counseling session or two.

Judy holds both of her hands up with fingers spread wide and her palms toward George.

"And someone, who shall remain nameless," she mocks, enunciating her words clearly, "stopped coming to our marriage counseling sessions."

"That nameless 'someone' didn't see the point of riding the memory-go-round one more time," George laments, rolling his head around in a circular motion. "No matter what we did, we couldn't cut through the hostility."

"And whose hostility are you referring to?" Judy snaps.

George blanches and turns away.

"Now who's playing the blame game? Why did you stop there? Why didn't you just divorce me?"

"Oh, Judy. Why dredge all this stuff up again? We had a little girl at home. I loved her."

George pauses for a moment. "And I loved you. I still love you both."

"That's hard to believe," Judy declares, throwing her arms up in the air.

"You never *would* believe it," George replies, exasperated. "Do you know how frustrating that was? I tried to tell you and show you how much I love you. But the more I tried, the angrier you became." George shifts in his chair to face Judy straighter on. "If you are ready to deal with your insatiable anger, I'll stay and talk to Phil with you."

"You think my anger is about *you*?" Judy asks with an angry chuckle. "You always make everything all about *you*."

"Your anger was always *directed* at me. What was I supposed to think?"

"Forget it, George. You never even tried to understand."

"Words can't *describe* how hard I tried to understand," George fires back with increasing exasperation. "It felt as if you *wanted* to be angry with me." George catches himself getting angrier and puts a lid on it. "Look, Judy, I don't know if we'll have any better luck in this room now than we ever did. We've found a way to live together without yelling at each other. Can't that be enough?"

"We've found a way to live *alone* together," Judy corrects him. "Living with you is like living by myself, especially with Becca gone. She used to keep me company while you watched sports on TV or played golf."

"What's wrong with that?" George pleads. "I figured the less time you had to spend with me, the less angry I would make you."

"See?" Judy fires at George. "It's always all about you."

George stands and begins to leave. "Let's stay the course and count our blessings." George makes it only as far as the door before Judy stops him again with her words.

"Or cut our losses," she warns menacingly, barely moving her jaw as she speaks.

George turns slowly back toward Judy.

"Or cut our losses?" he inquires, tilting his head slightly. "That doesn't sound good to me."

Judy folds her arms across her chest again and turns away from him. "Well, it *feels* good to me."

George takes several steps toward Judy. "Now look here, Judy…"

Judy whips around to face him and holds her hand out like a traffic cop. George stops abruptly with her hand about an inch from his chest. "You can stop right there," Judy threatens. "We spent years sitting in this room, trying to work things out. But we've never tried to work things *through*. We only managed to sweep them under the rug where we couldn't see them."

George spreads his arms wide. "I love you, Judy. I may be a clumsy husband, but I try to show you."

Judy holds her left hand in the air with fingers spread apart. "Your flowers, your date nights, your making dinner," she mocks with saccharin tones as she counts on her outstretched fingers, "checking off your 'Honey-Do' list. It means nothing if you don't love me, which you obviously don't."

"How can you say that? We spent years in this room trying to get to the bottom of the hostility between us. But, for whatever reason, we couldn't break through. The hostility at this moment, like all the other hostility over the years, isn't helping anything."

"Oh, it's helping me more than you'll ever understand," Judy responds. "It's helping me more than going home right now will help."

"Oh, stop it. Stop this. We're fine."

"We're *not* fine. But I'm going to be."

"We've been married almost thirty years, Judy," George volleys back, raising his voice. "There is no need to blow a gasket tonight."

Judy steps toward George and stands face-to-face with him.

"I can't wait another day longer to blow my gasket. You've had this coming for a long time," she retorts, matching his volume and exceeding it. "Our family has issues to deal with and I'm not going to be bogged down or held back by *you* anymore. Becca needs our help, and I am going to give it to her."

"Becca has a husband," George counters. "Let them work it out. Let them come to this room and 'work things *through*.'" He uses air quotes to emphasize his point. "Maybe they'll succeed where we failed."

Judy sits back down on the sofa and waves off her husband. "Go watch your basketball game. You don't want to miss it by wasting time in this room. But I'm not sweeping things under the rug anymore. Becca has a life in front of her, a promising career of her own, and plenty of time for a family."

"Isn't that *her* choice?"

Judy stands again and turns toward George in a rigid posture.

"You bet it's her choice, and I'm going to make sure she makes it," Judy announces proudly.

George pauses to ponder for a moment, walks back to the wing chair, and sits again.

"Why so militant all of the sudden?" he asks genuinely. "Is that what this is about? Having the right to choose in this state doesn't guarantee making the right choice."

Judy plants her fists on her hips. "What do you know about it?"

"I'm glad we never thought of exercising our 'choice' where Becca was concerned."

"Oh, don't even go there, George. I was the one with the choice, not you. Becca's choice belongs to her, not her husband."

George exhales in defeat as he rises to his feet, exhausted. "I will leave the rest of this conversation to you and Phil," he surrenders. "If he ever shows up."

Judy retrieves her cell phone from her purse and presses on the screen a few times.

"Call Pastor Phil," she commands. A few moments go by. "I don't know what happened tonight, Pastor," she says into the phone. "But Judy and George are at the church waiting for you. Call me back when you get this message." She presses the screen again to end the call.

George takes a step toward Judy, grasps her upper arms gently, and leans in to kiss her. Judy stiffens and jerks her head away from him, folding her arms across her chest again. George sighs, reaches into his jacket pocket, pulls out a handkerchief, and offers it to his wife.

"Here's a handkerchief. I remember how these sessions used to make you cry."

Judy continues to look away.

"Keep it," she says curtly. "I won't shed any tears over this session."

George gently places the handkerchief on the sofa cushion and walks to the doorway. Judy says nothing to stop him this time. He pauses for a moment anyway and looks back at his wife for a beat.

Judy remains frozen, looking away from him.

"Are you coming?" he inquires.

"I have my own car."

"I'll see you at home," he says softly and walks out the door and down the hall, his footsteps echoing on the tile floor. Judy doesn't move until she hears the creak of the wooden door opening and closing. She starts toward the door as if to catch George but then stops. She turns back toward the sofa and picks up the handkerchief George left there. She looks back toward the door then walks out into the hall, but, instead of turning right toward the exterior doors, she turns left and walks down the hallway, lit only by the light spilling from the classroom she just exited, to another set of double doors. She pulls one of the doors open and steps inside.

Judy stands at the back of a cavernous sanctuary, which is softly lit by street lights outside, giving the tall stained-glass windows a colorful glow. The aisle before her slopes gently downward toward the altar with the red eternal flame suspended high above it from the vaulted ceiling. She looks around for a moment and begins to slowly walk down the aisle. There is no sound as she walks on the carpeted aisle, passing the long pews upholstered in the same blue fabric as the chairs in the classroom.

As Judy walks, she notices some images on the stained-glass windows: the infant Jesus in His mother's arms, the infant Jesus in the manger, the infant Jesus in the arms of Simeon and Anna at the Temple. Other stained-glass images show little children coming to the adult Jesus as He sits and welcomes them. Judy looks at the stained-glass images as though she is seeing them for the first time. Reaching the chancel area, Judy pauses beneath the red lantern high above her head and looks up at it. She then turns and walks toward the wooden baptismal font.

Judy gently runs her hand over the wooden cover of the font, complete with a cross on top. Slowly, she pushes the cover aside and stares down at the water inside. Gingerly, she reaches down and runs one of her hands through the water. Cupping her hand, Judy allows the water to run through her fingers. Suddenly, she is overcome with emotion and quickly backs away from the font, leaving the lid open. She dries her hand with George's handkerchief and takes a few steps to the front row of pews and sits down. Holding the handkerchief to her face, she weeps softly at first and then sobs.

With tears streaming down her face, Judy looks up at the cross above the altar for about a minute, breathing heavily. She then looks down, closes her eyes, and shakes her head back and forth as if to shake thoughts out of her mind. Her sobbing lightens to soft weeping. She occasionally wipes her tears away. Then she rubs the handkerchief against her cheek and lays on her side in as much of a fetal position as she can manage on the pew, facing the altar. Judy inhales a deep breath through her nose and exhales a sigh from her mouth. As she lies there, her breathing becomes softer and more regular.

PART TWO

"Behold, I was brought forth in iniquity,
and in sin did my mother conceive me."
Psalm 51:5 (ESV)

As Judy slumbers in her fetal position on the front pew of the church, a figure appears behind her and casts a shadow over her. A hand reaches down and gently shakes Judy's shoulder.

"Judy," a young woman's voice calls to her. Judy doesn't awaken.

The shadow moves away.

Again, a hand reaches out and gently taps Judy's shoulder. A young woman dressed in slacks and a sweater is now standing in front of Judy, studying her closely. "Judy," the young woman calls out again, a little louder this time. "Judy, wake up."

Judy awakens with a start and sits up.

"You nearly gave me a heart attack," Judy gasps, looking around to see where she is. "It's about time somebody showed up. Where's Pastor Phil?"

"I'm so glad you came tonight," the young woman smiles. "Phil is at the arena downtown watching the game."

Judy studies the young woman up and down for a moment.

"I believe this church is being taken over by children," Judy snarls. "Everybody running this place looks so young now. Did you see my husband, George, on your way in?"

"You and I are the only ones in the building," the young woman answers. "Was he here with you and then left?"

Judy rolls her eyes. "He went home to watch the game on TV."

"He'll be back," the young woman assures her.

"What makes you say that?"

"You know how sometimes you just 'get a feeling'?" the young woman asks encouragingly.

"I don't care if he comes back or not," Judy pouts.

"What makes you say that?" The young woman's encouraging tone shifts to curiosity.

"You just missed our usual squabble. If you'd heard what he said to me, you wouldn't ask."

The young woman turns toward the altar, steps up a level, and picks up a chair identical to the contemporary wooden chairs in the classroom, but less worn. As she turns back toward Judy, she pauses just a moment to glance toward the still-open baptismal font. Her eyes shift back to Judy before she steps down and sets the chair on the floor facing Judy.

"May I sit with you?" she asks.

"It's *your* session," Judy says flatly.

"This session belongs to you, Judy. Not me." The young woman sits and extends her hands for Judy to grasp. "Can we pray first?"

Judy looks somewhat perplexed.

"I, I guess so."

The young woman reaches out and takes Judy's hands in hers. "Oh, Father God. Only You know why things happen the way they do. Only You know *how* things truly happen. We pray that You will fill this place and fill our hearts with Your Holy Spirit and that we will be guided by Your wisdom in what is about to be said — by both of us. In Jesus' name, Amen."

"Amen," Judy repeats with a slight hesitation in her voice.

The young woman smiles at Judy. "I thought you might want to talk for a bit, if that's all right?"

The two women exchange a long glance. The young woman continues to smile softly with eyes wide as she waits for Judy to speak.

Judy, a bit restless, sighs. "I was expecting Pastor Phil," she finally says with disappointment in her voice. "But talking will probably help me out somehow, no matter *who* it is." Judy looks down at George's handkerchief in her lap. "This night of all nights."

"Is there anything specific you want to talk about this evening?" the young woman coaxes. "Anything on your heart?"

"Yes, there is," Judy says matter-of-factly. "As long as we're here." Judy begins to tear up and sniffle again. She dabs her eyes with George's handkerchief.

"How are you feeling?"

"All of a sudden, out of nowhere, I feel like crying," Judy sniffs. "That's not like me."

"That looks like a man's handkerchief," the young woman observes.

"It's George's. For some reason, he thinks I cry in these sessions."

"It sounds like your journey has been difficult," the young woman comforts Judy.

Instead of feeling comforted, Judy suddenly stops sniffling and bristles.

"I'd say you are clairvoyant," Judy mocks. "But anyone with half a brain could have figured that out."

The young woman gently ignores Judy's rude remark. "What would you be doing right now if you weren't crying?" she asks.

"I'd be cursing the ground my husband walks on," Judy says angrily. "I'd be suing him for all the years of my life I have wasted on him. All the years I've lost because of his *selfishness.*"

"If you could get back all of those years you lost, what would you do differently?"

"I would marry somebody other than him," Judy snorts as if her point should have been obvious to the young woman. "Sure, George works hard, we have a good lifestyle with our combined incomes, but we could be having a lot more fun. We could be trying to wring out whatever dribs and drabs of youth we have left in these tired bodies." Judy holds George's handkerchief in her hands and wrings it out as if it were a wet dish rag.

The young woman perks up a little. "What does that word 'fun' mean to you?"

"You know, fun," Judy repeats again as if the young woman should have known. "Being really alive."

The young woman, even more curious now, leans forward in her chair toward Judy. "What does it feel like to be really alive?"

Judy looks a little crosswise at the young woman. "To be young again," Judy answers, now getting a bit whimsical. "Carefree, without boundaries, without burdens, without doubts..." Judy grins and nods as she recollects earlier days.

The young woman sits in the silence with her. After a moment, Judy looks at the young woman and smiles wistfully. The young woman smiles as well.

"Freedom came so naturally back then," Judy goes on. "But we protected our freedom. We didn't allow anything to hold us back or get in our way." Another long silence follows during which the young woman's smile gradually diminishes into a muted expression. "That was a lifetime ago."

The young woman nods her head slowly, gently.

"Now, all of a sudden," Judy restarts, "I'm desperate for it again. And George couldn't care less. Give him dinner and a soft place to watch a game on TV, and he's happy as a clam."

"If you knew then what you know now," the young woman asks, "what would you do differently?"

Judy doesn't hesitate. "I'd open my options again."

"How did marrying George affect your options?"

Judy stands and gestures in the air as if to illustrate. "That was the proverbial passage – the major life transition. There comes a time in life when you're supposed to settle down, get a real job, get married, have babies..." Judy pauses briefly. "...grow old." Judy looks at the young woman. "You'll be that age someday. It will sneak up behind you when you're not looking. The turning point. The tipping point. When I reached my tipping point, I stored my fantasies of freedom in my secret magic box where I could take them out when George was in the midst of clumsy love-making or in special, quiet, lonely times when he was playing golf or away on business." Judy sighs the sigh of lost youth. "We lost interest in each other a long time ago."

Judy pauses again and looks directly at the young woman. "I probably shouldn't be saying these things in a church building, should I?"

"If it's not appropriate to talk about scriptural behavior here," the young woman offers, "where is it appropriate to talk about it?"

Judy appears puzzled by the young woman's response. "Scriptural behavior?"

"God understands these impulses, Judy. Why do you think He gave us marriage?"

"I know God gave us marriage," Judy blurts as if the young woman has asked a silly question. "But what does marriage have to do with sexual thoughts?"

"God wanted the union between a man and a woman to be both spiritually *and* physically fulfilling."

"How do you know that?" Judy scoffs.

"God gave us erotic poetry," the young woman explains. Judy looks at the young woman blankly. The young woman extends her hand as if envisioning a scene in the distance over Judy's shoulder. "Your two breasts are like two fawns, twins of a gazelle, that feed among the lilies," the young woman recites.

Judy turns and follows where the young woman is looking to see if she can locate what she is describing. Seeing nothing, Judy turns back toward the young woman and tilts her head to the side inquisitively.

The young woman looks up at Judy and sees that she has lost her. "The Song of Solomon – chapter four, verse five."

Judy contemplates this last comment for a moment, wags her head from side to side, and sits back down. "I don't think George ever read the Old Testament. But God also said all that stuff about being responsible and treating my body as a holy temple."

"That's right," the young woman approves. "But He wouldn't have said it all unless He also gave us marriage."

"What about *before* marriage?" Judy asks sheepishly.

"How did you protect your holy temple while you had a desire to live fantasies?"

"What a question," Judy comments as if she's never considered it. She contemplates for a moment as the young woman waits patiently. "I guess I did protect it, for the most part. But I always wanted to live free. I never stopped having desires." Judy grabs hold of George's handkerchief by the corners and wraps it around her fingers on both hands and stretches it tight. "The best I could do was to white-knuckle my libido into submission."

"What would it be like if you had that again?" the young woman asks.

Judy looks at her quizzically like before. "A libido?"

The young woman smiles sheepishly at Judy's comment. "I mean, had a chance to live free again."

Judy finally gets it and relaxes a bit. "I know some women my age who are just beginning to embrace their fifty shades of everything, doing everything they can to be eighteen again. To me, that's a spiritual struggle that no one ever completely escapes. Even Jesus was tempted."

The young woman smiles and tilts her head slightly as Judy ponders for another moment.

"I can honestly say that, for the most part, my better angels stood their ground," Judy announces proudly.

"Are you happy your better angels stood their ground?"

"For the most part."

"For the most part?" the young woman probes deeper.

"Only with the most special kind of person in the most special moment..." Judy's voice drifts off as she seems to lose herself in a memory. "You could say this is a special anniversary for the most passionate, and painful, memories in my life." She takes George's handkerchief, sniffs, and dabs with it again.

The young woman watches her compassionately. "Are those memories connected?" the young woman inquires softly.

Despite how gently the question was asked, the young woman's question snatches Judy out of her memory and back into the church pew. Judy blinks, looks toward the young woman, and returns to the moment, apparently caught off guard – as if the young woman knows more than Judy thinks she should. Judy studies the young woman a little more closely with a hint of suspicion in her eyes.

"Have we ever met?" Judy presses.

"Not face-to face."

Judy seems mostly satisfied with the answer. "You know I never ever talk about this openly. Not even to my girlfriends. And certainly not to George."

The young woman seems encouraged. "Thank you for sharing with me," she says, lightening the mood.

"I'm very comfortable talking to you. Have you been a counselor for a long time?"

It's the young woman's turn to be caught off guard. She sits back in her chair and crosses her legs more formally as a counselor might.

"Do you have any children?" the young woman asks, avoiding Judy's question.

"I have a daughter," Judy offers.

The young woman perks up. "What's her name?"

"Becca."

The young woman can't help but lean forward again with a smile. "Please, tell me about her."

"Becca's a good girl, very smart, married to a nice-looking young man from a good family." Judy studies the young woman again. "Are *you* married?"

"I'm married to Jesus," the young woman says proudly with an air of deep assurance in the way she pronounces the name "Jesus," her smile widening.

Judy looks a bit surprised. "Are you a nun?"

"No," the young woman chuckles as if to suggest there are other ways to relate to Jesus.

"I've read about single Christian women who claim they've married Jesus," Judy supplies. "I suppose it would be very different from being married to George."

The young woman smiles and nods her head as if to confirm Judy's supposition.

Judy sinks back into the pew and studies the young woman some more. "How old are you?"

"I *would* be thirty."

"...*would* be thirty...?" Judy repeats with a forced British accent. "That sounds a bit Downton Abbey, don't you think? 'I *would* be thirty'?"

"How old is Becca?" the young woman moves on without acknowledging the British accent.

Judy waves George's handkerchief in the air in a distinctly eloquent Downton Abbey sort of way. "Becca *would be* twenty-five."

"Please, tell me more about her." The young woman continues, her curiosity growing as she leans into Judy even more.

Judy appears to enjoy talking about herself and her family. "Well, she's pretty like her mom," Judy says with a certain whimsy in her voice. "She has the whole world in front of her. She and her husband both have good jobs with lots of upside potential. They're getting a quick start on success."

"Like you and George did?" the young woman asks, obviously enjoying the tour of Judy's life.

"Yes, George and I thought we had the world on a string. At least at first. Especially as we walked down this very aisle." Judy turns and glances back at the center aisle of the church.

"At what point did George turn into a basketball fan?" the young woman asks.

"George was always a sports fan. Any sport. That's just a guy thing."

"Is that how you felt when he left tonight to watch the game?"

Judy pops back to her feet, takes a couple steps to her left, and turns back toward the young woman.

"No. I thought *that* was rude."

"It sounds as if you and Becca are like mother, like daughter," the young woman offers in hopes of distancing Judy from a sore subject.

Judy folds her arms and strokes her chin with her right hand. "I suppose we are," she replies, happy to be off of the subject of George.

"And Becca's husband and George are like..."

"Becca's husband and George are nothing alike," Judy blurts out, cutting the young woman off. "And George had nothing to do with it."

Judy's sudden explosion startles the young woman.

"Had nothing to do with what?"

"Why he and I come here to counsel with Pastor Phil. George and I spent years down the hall getting marriage counseling because I got pregnant. That's when our world dropped off the string." Judy becomes contemplative. "And George never could tie the world back onto the string for me. Lord knows he tried. He still tries."

"Then why are you so angry with him?"

Judy snaps out of her contemplation and sits back in the pew. "That's *your* job. You're the counselor. You figure it out and tell *me*."

"I hope we'll figure it out *together*," the young woman says invitingly.

Judy's tone becomes slightly sharper.

"Do you have children?"

"No."

"Have you ever been pregnant?"

"No."

"A fat lot of help you're going to be," Judy sighs.

"What did it feel like when you first became pregnant?" Judy jumps to her feet again as if launched with compressed air.

"I felt confused. Cheated. Tricked. Just when my life was getting on track; boom, derailed, train wreck." Judy deflates a little.

"Were there any casualties?" the young woman pries.

Judy looks at the young woman even more suspiciously. "What is *that* supposed to mean?"

"Did anyone get hurt?"

"Of course not. Becca is fine. She and her husband are now expecting a baby of their own."

"Did being pregnant hurt *you?*" the young woman presses.

"*Of course not,*" Judy repeats with a sneer. "I just told you that Becca was a healthy, happy baby."

"And you? Are you a healthy, happy mom?"

The young woman has obviously crossed a line.

"Look, I don't know what's going on here, exactly," an agitated Judy ramps up, "but ever since we started talking, I've had a really strange sensation. Comfortable and uncomfortable at the same time. It's a creepy feeling."

The young woman takes a deep breath, lets it out slowly, and continues to listen.

"You know what I'm talking about." Judy accuses.

The young woman continues to listen without responding.

"Something is starting to bubble up inside me as we talk. 'How old is Becca?' You're about the same age. 'Tell me about Becca...' Why do you want to know? Why is Becca so important all of a sudden?"

Despite Judy's escalating anger, the young woman pushes deeper, obviously now with an agenda. "Was Becca's birth when your world dropped off the string?"

Judy snarls fiercely, "I want you to tell me what is going on here. Right now."

"What's going on in your *mind* right now?" the young woman pries deeper.

"Enough of this game or whatever it is you're playing," Judy shouts.

"What do you feel like *doing* right now?" the young woman inquires as if nearing a breakthrough of some kind.

"I feel like storming out of here and reporting you to the licensing board."

The young woman seems a bit surprised. "For asking questions?"

"For asking questions that make me feel horrible."

"Why do *my* questions make *you* feel horrible?"

Judy pounds on her heart. "The things you are asking about are things that no one should know but me." Judy switches gears slightly. "Did Pastor Phil share with you things I confided in him? Things I thought were confidential? Because, if he did, I'll have his credentials, too. He'll never preach or provide spiritual counseling in this or any other church again."

"I've never spoken to Pastor Phil," the young woman says matter-of-factly.

Judy turns away from the young woman and grabs a handful of her own hair.

"Will somebody tell me what is going on here? I'm going crazy!"

"You're not crazy, Judy," the young woman assures her.

Judy lets go of her hair, whips around, and points an accusing finger directly at the young woman. "Then *you're* crazy," Judy concludes. "One of us is crazy. I'm getting creepy feelings because you're a creepy person, and you're asking creepy questions.

"What about *me* makes *you* feel creepy?"

Judy sits back in the pew, all of her senses aroused, like a cat ready to pounce. "You came out of nowhere," Judy exclaims. "You know too much. You're way too familiar to me. I got comfortable with you too fast. You say that you don't know Pastor Phil. But you know where he is and what he's doing tonight. Who *are* you?"

"Like I said, I am hoping you and I can figure that out *together*," the young woman says with hope in her voice.

"Oh, real cute. You're being a smart-mouth brat the way Becca gets when she's trying to win an argument with me."

"Am I arguing with you?" the young woman asks under complete control.

"You're getting under my skin the way Becca does. Talking to you is like talking to her. Do you talk this way to *your* mother?"

"Apparently..." the young woman says as if stating the obvious.

Judy slowly and silently mouths the word "apparently" as she rises to her feet. "That's it! I don't know who you think you are or what you're trying to pull off here, but I am not your mother. And you are not my daughter. My daughter is at home with her husband."

Judy begins to storm up the long aisle.

The young woman leans forward in her chair and calls after her. "Do you believe such things are possible?"

Judy stops. "Do I believe *what* things are possible?" she demands over her shoulder.

"That you could be talking to your daughter," the young woman reasons.

"Of course not," Judy exclaims, throwing her hands above her head in obvious aggravation. "I just told you that my daughter is at home with her husband."

"Is it possible that speaking to me could be *like* speaking to your daughter?"

Judy contemplates for a moment before turning slowly back toward the young woman. "Oh, I get it," Judy says, exaggerating her mockery in a high-pitched voice as if she has stumbled into a major epiphany. "This is some kind of psychological empty chair exercise. Oh, no," she continues with exaggerated vocal inflection. "It can't be an empty chair exercise because the chair isn't empty. You're sitting in it." Judy snaps her fingers to announce another possibility. "Oh, I've got it. We're going to roleplay." You pretend to be Becca or George, and I will tell you everything I'm afraid to tell them to their face." The snideness in Judy's voice takes on a vicious edge. "Well. That might have been a fun psycho-babble game to play about ten minutes ago before I found out you're *insane*."

Judy turns to walk out again.

The young woman jumps to her feet.

"Do you believe that in Christ all things are possible?"

Again, Judy stops and responds without turning around. "Of course in Christ all things are possible. But with you, I am done."

She starts up the aisle again. "Good night," Judy says with a flick of her wrist in the young woman's direction.

"You never said that to me before," the young woman exclaims as if finding buried treasure in Judy's words.

Judy stops again, glancing down at the floor to her left. "Never said *what* to you before?"

The young woman takes a couple baby steps toward where Judy is standing. "Good night," she purrs, oozing sentimentality.

Judy turns slowly, takes a deep breath and walks menacingly to where the young woman is standing. Despite the smile on her face, the young woman flicks a tear from her eye.

Judy, practically nose-to-nose with the young woman, speaks in a deep, throaty voice. "Look, whoever you are, if this is a joke, it's a sick joke. If this is a hoax, it is the cruelest hoax ever. You are the meanest person I've ever met."

The young woman was apparently hoping for a different reaction from Judy. "Why do you say that?"

"Because you are, for whatever reason, pretending to be my first daughter."

"First daughter?" the young woman says with anticipation.

Judy rolls her eyes and her head as she shakes her fist in the air.

"I swear I'm going to kill Phil with my bare hands.

"What do you feel like doing right *now*?" the young woman's hopeful anticipation remains undiminished.

"Right now, I feel like killing *you*."

There is an awkward moment of silence as the two women stare into each other's eyes and the air escapes from the young woman's deflating hopefulness.

"I am sorry you feel that way," comes the young woman's soft response. "I'm sorry you *ever* felt that way."

Judy is not quite finished as she points her finger toward the young woman's heart. "This is pathetic. *You* are pathetic. My daughter is named Becca. I don't have another daughter. Capisce? I don't know who you are, and I don't know what you hoped to accomplish here tonight. But I am going home, and you haven't heard the last of this." Judy turns and takes another few steps up the aisle toward the door, then stops abruptly, turns, and takes one step back toward the young woman. There are now tears of wounded rage in Judy's eyes.

"I do not deserve to be treated this way," Judy declares. "What did I ever do to *you*?" With that, Judy turns on her heels and storms up the aisle and out, nearly pushing the door off its hinges in the process.

The young woman raises a hand as if to stop her but says nothing as the door closes itself behind Judy. The young woman stares at the doors for a long while, then walks to where Judy was sitting in the front pew. She runs her hand along the wooden top of the pew and then the blue upholstery where Judy was seated. The young woman turns, walks to the baptismal font, stares down into the water for a few moments, and glances toward the back of the sanctuary where Judy exited before she slowly closes the lid. She walks back to the front pew, plops down where Judy was sitting, and begins to sob. Still sobbing, the young woman rises and walks to the altar where she kneels, folds her hands, and looks up at the cross above as tears stream down her cheeks.

PART THREE

"You are in Christ; therefore, you cannot be denied."
2 Corinthians 5:17 (KJV)

As the young woman continues to weep, Judy steals back into the sanctuary and walks quietly down the aisle, stopping about halfway. She stands in silence and watches the young woman cry for a moment before she speaks.

"I would like to ask *you* some questions if you don't mind," Judy announces with a certain coyness in her voice.

Startled, the young woman jumps to her feet, smiling. "Of course," she blurts out while wiping tears away from both eyes and drying her hands on her slacks. "I'm so glad you came back."

Judy continues walking casually down the aisle. "I wouldn't be so sure of that if I were you."

The young woman moves to sit in her original seat across from the front pew.

"No, no," Judy corrects her. "Sit here." Judy pats the back of the front pew where the young girl first awakened her. The young woman walks to the pew and turns to sit. "We'll trade seats so I can interrogate…" Judy places her hand on the young woman's shoulder and pushes her down into the pew. "… *You.*"

Judy paces as she speaks, wringing her hands gently, and the young woman follows her back and forth with her eyes. "Since you seem to think I had a daughter before Becca," Judy interrogates, "tell me, when was she born?"

The young woman shifts in her seat nervously and says nothing. She wears a concerned expression.

"Oh, my," Judy feigns surprise. "Don't tell me you're going to fail your exam on the very first question. This one is so *easy*. All you have to do is search birth certificate records. Good grief. You are such an amateur. My advice to you is get your facts straight before you start making accusations. Good-bye."

As Judy turns to exit again, the young woman stands. "I'm not here to accuse you," the young woman pleads. "I'm here to talk to you."

Judy pauses but does not turn back toward the young woman. "Well, talk fast because I'm on my way out the door."

"Your first daughter was never born," the young woman explains. "She never had a birth certificate – or a death certificate."

Judy turns slowly to the young woman. "Am I supposed to be impressed with *that*? Just a detail that my 'confidential' counselor, Pastor Phil, obviously shared with you."

The young woman walks into the aisle and faces Judy head on. "I told you I've never met or spoken to Pastor Phil."

Judy shakes her head side-to-side as she speaks. "So now you're suggesting that I became pregnant with a female baby before Becca, and the first baby died?"

"I am suggesting that you became pregnant with a female baby before Becca, and she was *killed.* There's a difference."

"Who do you think you are?" Judy explodes. "One more comment like that and I'll slap you into next week."

The young woman does not flinch as she looks into Judy's furious eyes and straightens her spine.

"I'm just getting the *facts straight.*"

"How dare you insinuate that I would have my own child killed!" Judy shouts.

The young woman holds her ground. "Is that what I'm insinuating?" the young woman asks confidently with a slight head tilt of her own.

"Is there any other way a child can…" Judy stops suddenly as if she just realized she is in checkmate.

The two women glare at each other down for another few moments. Judy suddenly exhales a burst of air, begins to chuckle, and then throws her head back and laughs wickedly.

"Alrighty then." Judy chuckles some more as she strolls nonchalantly to the chair the young woman first sat in. "I'm really, really curious where you think you're going with this." Turning as if to sit in the chair, Judy suggests, "Let's continue the exam. When did this…" she sits properly, "…*homicide* take place?" Judy crosses her legs, sits forward, intertwines her fingers around her knee, and listens intently with a smirk on her face.

The young woman sits back down in the front pew and takes in a long, slow breath. "Thirty years ago, tonight," she answers calmly but clearly.

Judy releases her grip on her own knee and slowly lowers her foot to the floor. "I grant you Pastor Phil never knew that. Those records are sealed. It's discoverable though. Someone as devious as you could probably find out somehow."

"Am I passing the exam so far?" the young woman asks with raised eyebrows.

"Not with any information a con artist couldn't come up with," Judy counters.

"Ask me something that only your first daughter could know," the young woman continued.

"What?" Judy asks incredulously.

"Please, ask me something that only your first daughter could know," the young woman repeats.

"How could you possibly know something only my first daughter could know? Are you actually still sitting there trying to convince me that you're my first daughter?"

The young woman looks away in frustration.

"Look at me when I'm talking to you!" Judy shrieks.

The young woman looks back slowly and stares silently into Judy's eyes.

Judy glares back at the young woman, becomes flustered again, but then composes herself. Attempting to look relaxed, Judy leans back in the chair. "Okay, okay. Let's continue. Just for a moment more. What was it like for you that evening thirty years ago tonight?"

The young woman takes a deep breath and continues looking straight at Judy.

"That's right," Judy says, sensing she has turned the tables with a checkmate question of her own. "I know where you are going with this, and I am not going to run away. I'll play this charade as far as it goes. Were you *scared* thirty years ago tonight?"

The young woman exhales with a gush. "I wish this part weren't necessary," she moans.

Judy, sensing she is winning, moves in for the coup de grace. "Oh, but it *is*," she insists, ready to deal the death blow. "Let's play this little charade out to its dramatic climax. Use your imagination if you are staging this, which I think you are. Tell me how you experienced that evening, thirty years ago tonight." Judy crosses her legs again complete with the intertwined fingers around her knee. "Hm-m-m?"

The young woman takes a deep breath and speaks softly, choosing her words carefully. "You were nervous, anxious, frightened…"

Judy waves her hands to cut off the young woman. "Oh no you don't. Stop trying to turn this around. We're not talking about me," Judy makes clear by pointing at herself. "We're talking about *you.*" She turns her finger around to point it at the young woman. "It's your turn on the rotisserie."

"I felt the same raw emotions you felt," the young woman maintains. "In my pre-cognitive state, I didn't understand why I felt what I felt or the circumstances surrounding the emotional storm you were experiencing. But whatever chemicals were coursing through you that evening were coursing through me. We were still one biological system at that point."

"Nice try," Judy dismisses. "What did you say your name is…?"

"I didn't say."

Judy folds her arms. "Isn't that just a little rude?"

"I didn't tell you my name because you never gave me one," the young woman clarifies with a sad tone.

"Oh, you fight dirty," Judy sneers.

"I didn't come to fight with you."

"Then why did you come?"

"I came to give you your life back," the young woman exclaims.

"Oh, please," Judy protests. "My life is just fine. Never better. Answer my question. Tell me what happened that evening thirty years ago tonight. I have no recollection because I was anesthetized."

"So was I," the young woman points out.

"Oh no. You're not wiggling off this hook that easily. Use your wild imagination if need be. If you came here tonight from wherever dead babies go, the babies without birthdays – only death days – you *must* have God's cell number. If you can't remember, call and ask Him. What did they do to you?"

"Why do you ask me what you already know?" the young woman responds.

"What's that supposed to mean?" Judy sneers.

"You know what happened to me because you were so haunted by what you had done that, years later, you researched the medical techniques and procedures used to terminate the lives of the preborn," the young woman continues with increasing intensity. "You even talked to doctors who had performed those procedures before they abandoned the bloody business because they could no longer participate in something so cruel and brutal. If even the most hideous, reprehensible, violent, and deadly criminals on earth were executed with the methods used to kill and dismember preborn babies and extract their corpses from the womb, the public outcry would be deafening."

Judy begins to wag her head slowly from side to side.

"You even began to wake up in the middle of the night after dreaming about my helplessness and innocence, every maternal instinct in your body crying out for you to protect me."

"That's where you are wrong," Judy snaps back and with increasing animation. "I had loving counselors at the family planning clinic who educated and enlightened me. They explained that there was no 'baby' inside of me – only non-viable tissue. Non-viable tissue that could not survive on its own outside the womb. 'Helpless?' 'Innocent?' Non-viable tissue is not helpless. Non-viable tissue is not innocent. Non-viable tissue is *nothing*. Non-viable tissue can't feel anything because non-viable tissue *isn't anything*. That's why my abortion counselors told me not to give a name to medical waste."

The young woman is undeterred. "Did they show you an ultrasound of your baby? Did that look like medical waste to you?"

The young woman's question only angers Judy more. "What did I just say?" she bellows. "No, they didn't show me an ultrasound of my baby because there *was no baby!*"

The young woman stands, takes a few steps toward the altar and then turns back toward Judy.

"How in our God's creation," the young woman reasons, "could that living tissue, from the electric spark at the instant of conception, have been a life form other than human? How could that living tissue possibly have been another species? How could that living tissue have possibly been an ethnicity other than what you and my father were?" The young woman spreads out her arms and looks heavenward. "How could that living tissue have avoided being born if left to grow organically on life's natural journey?"

The young woman begins moving back toward Judy. "How is it medically, scientifically, or biologically possible for that tissue – that DNA fingerprint unique among all others on the planet – to ever have naturally become anything other than *me*?" The young woman holds her hands in front of Judy's face so she can examine her fingerprints.

Judy turns in her chair and looks away. "Sorry. Not having this conversation."

The young woman walks around so that she is again facing Judy as she presses onward. "How can you come here tonight and repeat with such eloquence what abortion facility counselors told you? They tried to convince you that natural science is not real – that embryologists have it all wrong. It's God's science, thank you, and the best that human 'scientists' can do is try to piece it together and figure it out."

Judy raises her hand to stop the young woman. "Before you bring God into this, let me remind you that one of my counselors at the family planning clinic was Lutheran. One of the nurses told me she was Presbyterian. Another nurse was someone *from this church!* They all told me not to worry – that God was totally fine with what I was doing – that He wanted me to live a full and abundant life. My best life now!" Judy draws in a long breath to reload as she slowly stands to confront the young woman nose-to-nose again. "They warned me that hateful people like you would come and try to shame me and steal my joy. And they were right." Judy waves her hand up and down in front of the young woman. "Here you are. Yes, I decided to believe their words and make them my own because they were kind and comforting from the moment I called for an appointment. They never tried to lay a guilt trip on me like you're trying to do. Their words and actions showed they cared for *me*, not some parasite. Their words kept me from ruining my life the way you're trying to ruin it right now."

"Please, please try to understand," the young woman pleads as she reaches out, and ever-so-gently touches Judy on the arm.

Judy recoils and retreats from the young woman, yanking her arm violently out of her reach.

"Don't you touch me!" Judy shrieks. "I suppose you're going to tell me about how your little heart was beating that night. Or how your little fetal brain was crying out, *Mommy, don't. Mommy, don't.*"

"You know perfectly well what they did to my fetal brain," the young woman states calmly and confidently.

Judy whips her head from side to side as if trying to shake off the entire conversation before running to the altar where she throws her head back and raises both her arms toward the cross crying out, "Dear God, why are You doing this to me?"

Judy then buries her face in her hands.

The young woman takes a small step toward Judy and straightens up as if she is about to attempt a difficult word at a spelling bee. "My Dearest Little One," the young woman recites tenderly. "You would have become an adult this year. I can never know which day would have been your birthday, but I know how old you would have been this year."

Judy begins to slowly lower her hands from her face as the young woman continues. "Who would you be now, Little One? A rebel like your mother? An adventurer like your father? A smarty pants like your little sister? I sometimes try to pretend that we are skipping through life's moments together. Your first Easter outfit... Your high school prom... But wondering these things only makes me weep. So, I must be as brave as I imagine."

Judy lets her arms fall limp at her sides and takes in a long breath. She stares up at the cross above her as she mouths the words of the next sentence as the young woman speaks them aloud.

"You were never a choice, Little One. You have always been my precious child. Your loving mother."

There is a long silence. Judy continues to look up at the cross above the altar. "I burned that letter the moment I finished it," Judy reveals in a defeated tone.

"On the 21st anniversary of my death," the young woman adds.

"Yes," Judy confirms. "Nine years ago, today."

"And you spread the ashes at the base of the maple tree you planted beside the house on the tenth anniversary."

"Yes."

"It's a beautiful tree," the young woman acknowledges with a smile. "Thank you."

Judy turns slowly, walks to where the young woman is standing, reaches out, lifts the young woman's chin with her fingertips, and looks into her eyes. Judy tilts her head from side to side slightly as she studies the young woman's eyes.

The young woman returns a soft glance.

Judy exhales a big breath of resignation. "Who would have ever thought that you would have your father's eyes?" Judy says gently. "But why wouldn't you? This is the first time I've ever looked into your eyes. They look exactly as I have always imagined them."

PART FOUR

Judy lets her hand gracefully fall away from her daughter's chin and sits back down in the chair. "You never had to say a word to win our little argument."

The young woman returns to her seat in the pew and reaches over to touch Judy gently on the knee. "But you *did.*"

"I knew who you might be ten minutes after you woke me," Judy confesses. "You know how sometimes 'you just get a feeling'?" Judy echoes the young woman's words from a few minutes after she was first awakened.

"You had three decades of lies to dig out from under," her daughter acknowledges.

Judy begins to cry, wag her head slowly, and shake. She slips off the chair and sinks to her knees in front of her daughter. "No one warned me that my heart would break every morning or how much I would miss a nameless blob of non-viable tissue every day of my life. Women can grieve a lifetime after a miscarriage or a stillbirth. How could I have let them convince me that I wouldn't grieve after aborting my own child? Even after Becca was born, I still missed the big sister she doesn't even know she has." Judy pounds on the floor with her fist. The young woman stands and reaches down to comfort her.

"Why are you doing this?" Judy wails. "Why are you doing this? They *promised* me this would never happen. They promised me!" Judy continues to sob and gasp for breath as she reaches out and wraps her arms around her daughter's legs, hugging her tight. "They lied to me..."

The young woman kneels down facing Judy and tenderly cradles Judy's face in her hands. Slowly she kisses Judy's cheeks one at a time.

Suddenly, Judy throws her arms around her daughter's neck and hugs her tight. "I'm sorry. I'm sorry. I'm sorry."

The young woman gently rocks her mother side to side, and when Judy's sobbing slowly subsides, the young woman takes George's handkerchief from Judy's hand and dabs the tears from her mother's eyes. The young woman holds the handkerchief out for Judy who takes it, sits back on her heels, and continues to dry the tears from her eyes.

"I guess George was right," Judy says softly.

"Right about what?" her daughter asks.

"I *do* cry at these sessions."

Both women blurt out a giggle that pierces the crying. The young woman sits back on her heels as well and brushes away her own tears with the backs of her hands. When Judy notices this, she uses George's handkerchief to dab lovingly at her daughter's tears before shifting to sit on the floor. Judy extends her legs in front of her and gently guides her daughter's head into her lap. Judy looks down at her daughter, gently playing with her hair.

"Can you stay with me?" Judy asks.

The young woman shifts so that she can look straight up into her mother's eyes. "For a little while," she assures her.

"Tonight was not your fault," Judy returns her daughter's assurance. "None of this was your fault. As I started to suspect who you really are, suddenly it all began to make sense. The phantom text messages. The empty building. And the fact that you look so very much like your father. I hope you understand. I had to fight the truth as hard as I could for as long as I could. The lies kept me alive for thirty years."

The young woman looks up at Judy. "The lies were all you had to cling to. I know that. All you had to do was make peace with your choice. Or so you thought."

Despite the tears, a smile creeps across Judy's face. "Or so I thought. Until you came." Judy tenderly strokes her daughter's face with her fingers. "I never thought I would stare into his eyes again." Judy takes her index finger and touches the tip of her daughter's nose. "You got my nose though."

The young woman scrunches her nose at her mother, Judy does the same and bends forward to touch noses with her daughter. They both giggle. Judy begins to play with her daughter's hair again. "Are your features, your hair, your eyes...is what I am seeing and touching real?

The young woman nods her head. "Yes."

There is more silence as Judy studies her daughter's face and body, right down to the young woman's toes. Judy holds her daughter's hand and studies it, front and back, kissing each fingertip one-by-one.

"Am I really holding your 30-year-old hand?" The young woman nods her head again. Judy gazes up toward the cross above the altar and then closes her eyes. "Oh, in Christ, all things *are* possible." Judy kisses the palm of the young woman's hand and then presses it against her own cheek and inhales a deep, deep breath, releasing a few more sobs. Judy looks back down into her daughter's eyes. "Are you an angel?"

The young woman smiles and looks up at her mother. "No. I'm human."

After a pause, "Do you hate me?" Judy wonders aloud, turning her head away and pinching her eyes closed to hold back what could be a flood of tears.

While Judy's eyes are closed, anticipating the answer, the young woman reaches up and caresses the side of Judy's face. Without opening her eyes, Judy seals her lips tight, breathes through her nose, and tilts her head back as her chest heaves and she fights to hold in everything that could burst forth at any moment.

The young woman continues to caress the side of Judy's face.

"Hush now," the young woman comforts. Judy fights back the explosion harder than ever. "Hush."

The young woman gently caresses Judy's chin and tilts her mother's face downward.

"Hey..."

Judy looks down into her daughter's eyes.

"I love you," the young woman assures her mother. Judy wraps her arms around her daughter and squeezes tight, allowing a couple more sobs to escape.

"Is that what you came back from the dead to tell me?"

"I didn't come back from the dead."

"But I had you killed. You said so yourself."

"My soul wasn't killed," the young woman says assuringly. "No human can do that. Our souls are immortal."

"But..." Judy protests.

The young woman reaches her hand up and places her index finger over her mother's lips. "Yes, I am here to tell you I love you. More importantly, I am here to tell you that *Jesus* loves you and that you are forgiven and set free."

Judy takes her daughter's hand and rubs it against her own cheek again.

"Oh, I love you. I love you so-o-o much. Through all these years, not a day has gone by without a thought of you – a prayer for you. I wanted so much to hold you and hoped so hard that you were in Heaven. Do you live in Heaven?" Judy begins to rock her daughter gently.

The young woman reaches up and clasps Judy's hand in her own, squeezing tightly. "Stop. God is loving, just, and merciful. He is amazing, and He will answer all your questions in His time."

Judy gazes at her daughter, soaking her in for a few more moments. "You are more beautiful than I could have ever imagined. Would you have gotten along with your sister, Becca?"

The young woman sits up, pulls her knees to her chest, wraps her arms around her knees, and turns toward her mother. "God doesn't deal in hypotheticals."

"But..." Judy protests again.

The young woman holds her hand up as a signal for her mother to pause. "No more questions. We are who we are. We are what we are.

We are here now because of the choices we make and, sometimes, the choices that are made for us."

Judy looks away sadly.

"Don't be sad. He isn't. He brought us together. That was *His* choice. Heaven is rejoicing for you at this very moment."

"When will I see you again?" Judy probes, missing the enormity of what her daughter is sharing with her. "If our souls never die, then..."

The young woman gets to her feet.

"I'm sorry," Judy apologizes. "I didn't mean to talk your ear off. Now I've upset you." Judy reaches up and strokes her daughter's forearm.

The young woman shakes her head as she clasps Judy's hands in her own and helps her mother to her feet. The two women stand facing each other, and the young woman strokes her mother's upper arms. "Whenever you feel desperate to know something, ask *Him*. He will reveal whatever you need to know, in His time, and not a moment too soon or too late."

"Why, though?" Judy inquires, looking puzzled.

"Why...?"

"Why this? Why you? Why me? Why now?" Judy completes her question.

The young woman sighs. "God wants you to know that you're completely free. He allowed His own child to be put to death so that you don't need to feel guilty or ashamed for what you did to yours. There is no condemnation in His heart for you any more than there is for me. Jesus wants you to experience His complete love and indescribable joy."

"Even after what I did?" Judy is obviously not familiar with a life without self-condemnation.

"No matter *what* you do," the young woman assures her mother. "As long as you confess it, surrender your life to Him, accept Him as your personal Lord and Savior, and abide in Him always, you will live in His presence and His peace forever. No one will ever be able to take you or me out of the palm of His almighty, everlasting hand. Our Father in Heaven no longer even sees what you did. Jesus left those memories nailed to the cross."

"Will I ever see you again?" Judy asks with anticipation in her voice.

The young woman smiles confidently. "Remain in Him and He will remain in you…forever. And so will I." The young woman lays her palm over Judy's heart. "Right here." The young woman then reaches out and holds both of her mother's hands. "We'll see each other again soon enough."

Judy breathes deeply several times as as they stand facing each other. Suddenly, Judy embraces her daughter fully, and the young woman wraps her arms around her mother. After a long moment, they step back from each other, still holding hands. A sympathetic smile crosses the young woman's lips. She kisses her mother's right cheek. As the young woman starts to back away, Judy holds tightly onto both of her hands.

"Must you…? There's so much more I want to know. We have a lifetime to catch up on."

The young woman stares back at her mother and slowly shakes her head from side to side.

"Oh, that would be hypothetical, wouldn't it?" Judy acknowledges, suggesting that she is beginning to better comprehend the message her daughter is trying to deliver. The young woman nods her head approvingly.

"We've had the talk I came to have with you. If you feel lonely for me, guilty for what happened, or have a question, don't write a letter like you did before, or try to contact me, just go to your knees and take it to the Lord in prayer. That's what God wants, to have a conversation directly with you. Lay everything at the foot of the cross, especially me." The young woman motions toward the cross above the altar. "And *He* will comfort you."

The young woman hesitates for a moment and then kisses Judy tenderly on her other cheek and on both of her hands. Judy begins to cry again. "Good-bye, Judy. Use your suffering for God's glory." The young woman begins to back away. But Judy grasps her daughter's hands a little tighter.

"Please say it the right way," Judy pleads. "For me. I want to hear you say it in *your* voice."

The young woman leads Judy the few steps to the altar and motions for her to kneel. Judy does. The young woman also kneels, takes George's handkerchief from Judy, and dabs her mother's tears one last time. The young woman wipes away a few of her own tears, kisses the handkerchief, and holds it out to her mother. Judy accepts it in the palm of her hand. The young woman closes her mother's hands around the handkerchief and stands. Still kneeling, a smile of resignation creeps across Judy's lips. Her daughter motions to the cross and turns her mother's head toward it.

"Everything you will ever need is right here. This is where you always will find me. Don't look back. Just gaze on His sacrifice." The young woman gently tilts her mother's head back and looks down into her eyes.

"Good night…mother." The young woman kisses her mother's forehead and then backs away slowly. Judy gasps with joy, looks up to the cross, and closes her eyes.

"Good night, Little One," Judy calls out tenderly without turning. "I love you."

PART FIVE

*"Brothers and sisters, if someone is caught in a sin,
you who live by the Spirit should restore that person gently."*
Galatians 6:1 (NIV)

Judy lies curled in a fetal position in front of the altar, George's handkerchief still clutched between her hands. A human shadow once again casts over her slumbering body. As before, a hand reaches out and touches her on the shoulder.

"Judy?"

Judy stirs but doesn't wake up. The hand reaches down, takes Judy's hand, and pats it gently.

"Judy? Wake up, honey."

Judy blinks a few times and opens her eyes to see that she is holding George's hand.

Still groggy from sleeping, she says, "Oh, it's you." She sounds a little disappointed. Becoming more lucid, Judy asks, with more energy,

"Did you see her on your way in?" She sits up, tilts her head, and looks around George up the aisle behind him, first one way and then the other.

"See who?"

Judy stands up, tugging on George's hand to help herself stand. George assists her with both hands.

"The young woman who was here," Judy explains, looking around the shadowy sanctuary.

"What woman? The church is still dark and empty. You and I are still the only ones in the building."

"After you left, a young woman came in," Judy recollects.

"Phil never showed up?"

"No. Just the young woman." Judy looks into Geroge's eyes briefly. "She…" Judy stops herself. "She was a church counselor," she semi-stutters, her voice trailing off. "She was sitting right there." Judy points toward the blue upholstered chair facing the front pew, only to see that it is next to the altar, back in its original place before the young woman moved it. Judy lets go of George's hand and walks slowly over to the chair, looks at it for a moment, then reaches down and touches the seat. George watches with a puzzled look on his face as Judy glances toward the baptismal font, the lid of which is closed. She walks over to it, slides the top open, looks inside the silver basin, then leans forward slightly for a closer look. She reaches in and runs her finger along the bottom of the basin, raises her fingers in front of her face, and rubs them together. They are dry.

"What are you doing, Judy?"

Judy looks at George, her fingers still pinched together in front of her face. She looks back at the font, reaches down, and taps the bottom of the empty stainless-steel basin with her fingernail twice.

Bink, bink.

She slowly slides the lid closed. Judy studies the closed lid on the baptismal font for a couple more moments.

"How did you end up in here?" George continues.

Judy looks back at George. "How did *you* end up in here?"

"Looking for you. I didn't find you in the other room, but your purse and coat are still in there. I was worried and then had a hunch that you might be in here."

Judy looks around the cavernous sanctuary of the church briefly before glancing up at the eternal flame, glowing in its red lantern high above the altar. She looks back at George, takes a deep breath, and says, "Let's go back into the other room."

George holds his arm out for her to take. She looks at it for a moment and then wraps her arm in his. She remains expressionless as they begin to walk up the aisle together toward the double doors.

"Are you finished with that?" George asks, reaching for the hand-kerchief in her hand.

Judy stops abruptly and holds the handkerchief out of his reach.

"I don't think I will ever let this out of my sight," she says with conviction.

"Okay," George says apologetically as if to de-escalate whatever land-mine he might have inadvertently stepped on. He withdraws his reach slowly, avoiding any sudden moves.

They resume their walk up the aisle silently and get about halfway to the double doors, Judy stops and looks back down the aisle to-ward the altar. "Do you remember walking down this aisle all those years ago?"

George glances back toward the altar as well. "Like it was yesterday," he says sentimentally.

Judy begins walking again, still holding George's handkerchief in her hand.

George holds one of the double doors open for Judy as they pass through and walk in silence down the hall to the classroom, where light spills into the dark hallway. The only sound in those few mo-ments is the faint splashing of cars on the rainy street outside. George motions for Judy to enter the room first, but she hesitates in the doorway before walking in.

"You came back," Judy observes, turning toward George.

"Yeah, I'm not sure why," George says with uncertainty in his voice.

Judy fiddles again with the handkerchief in her hand as she walks back to the sofa where she was seated earlier. She reaches down and picks up her purse, which is exactly where she left it.

"Because she said you would," Judy says.

"She? Who is *she?*" George demands. "The counselor?"

Judy nods her head.

"What was her name?"

George's question causes Judy to pause.

"I never gave her one," Judy says reminiscently.

George remains at the doorway. "What do you mean, 'You never gave her one'?"

Judy pauses for a beat, sits, sets down her purse, and motions for George to join her on the sofa. "Sit." Judy pats the cushion next to her.

"Sit as in 'I'm about to pinch your head off'? Or 'Sit, we have much to discuss'?"

Understanding George's hesitation, Judy smiles reassuringly and continues to pat the seat cushion next to her on the sofa. "Just sit, George."

George walks over and sits cautiously on the opposite end of the sofa. "Did this counselor explain to you how or why everything got so weird with the text messages, the empty building, or Phil?"

Judy smiles. "I guess you could say she helped me understand."

"Can you help *me* understand?"

"Why *did* you come back, George?"

"I told you. I don't *know* why."

"I think you do," Judy says, playing with George's handkerchief in her hands.

George shifts uncomfortably and looks at Judy for a moment. "You're right. I do." There is resignation in George's voice. "After I went home earlier, I couldn't get settled. I couldn't focus on the game. And I fell asleep."

"That's not like you to fall asleep during a game..."

"I know," George says as if Judy had just made the most obvious observation possible. "We were behind by *two points* when I fell asleep. I didn't know what was bothering me, but I woke up with a sense that the answer to the mysterious text messages and the unlocked door to a dark and empty building was here."

"Did we win the game?" Judy queries.

George shakes off her question. "I don't know. But it doesn't matter."

Judy's eyes grow as round as saucers. "What did you expect to find?"

"You. Maybe Phil. Did *you* get answers?"

Judy rolls her eyes. "More than you know."

"Care to share?"

Judy hesitates and looks long into George's eyes.

George raises his eyebrows anticipating an answer.

Judy takes a deep breath. "This might not be a good idea, George."

"Whoa," George protests. "All those times we sat in this room with Phil when he was bugging me to share more. You were bugging me to share more. Now, when the shoe is on the other foot, you clam up. That feels really unfair."

Judy looks again into George's eyes and takes another long breath. "Can we pray first?" she asks as if padding for time. She reaches her hands out to George.

He again looks a little perplexed, but nonetheless leans toward his wife and holds his hands out to her. "I guess so."

Judy grasps his hands in her own. George bows his head and closes his eyes suspiciously. Prayer is not a common practice for the two of them, especially on her initiation. Judy bows her head and closes her eyes.

"Please, Lord," Judy begins, "let me be a speaker of the truth, Your truth. Protect my heart and protect George's heart."

George shifts in his seat, raises his head, opens his eyes, looks at Judy, and then around the room.

Not noticing, Judy continues, "Give us a spirit of understanding. Let us practice mercy and grace in the same way You extend mercy and grace to us. In Jesus' name…"

Hearing the prayer is about to end, George closes his eyes and quickly bows his head.

"Amen," Judy concludes.

George gingerly pulls his hands away from Judy's, looks up at her, and then repeats, "Amen." The curiosity in his voice is evident. "So, is this the end for us?" he continues. "Is that what the prayer was about? A pre-apology? Did you and the counselor decide you're better off without me? That's where you were headed when I was leaving."

"I can certainly understand why your mind would go there, George. But I hope this is not the end for us. The more relevant question might be: Are you better off without *me?*"

George shakes his head in frustration. "Is that another way of saying, 'It's not you, it's me. But I'm leaving anyway'? Please tell me straight out. Where do we stand?"

"I can tell you straight out where I stand," Judy offers.

George sits back, crosses his legs, and folds his arms across his chest. "Well? I'm listening..."

Judy closes her eyes and inhales a long breath through her nose. "I had an abortion," she exhales, opening one eye to monitor George's reaction.

George slowly unfolds his arms and lowers his crossed leg to the floor as an astonished expression possesses his face. "Say that again," he says as if he doesn't believe what he just heard.

Judy looks away to summon more courage and then turns back to look George in the eyes.

"I had an abortion," she repeats more boldly.

"When exactly did this happen?" George probes. "I don't want to sound mean, but aren't you already post-menopausal?"

Judy rolls her eyes.

"Come on, truth speaker, when did this happen?" There is a hint of sarcasm in George's voice. Judy steels herself. "Thirty years ago, tonight."

George rises to his feet, speechless. He starts back toward the bookshelf counting on his fingers, turns back toward Judy, begins to say something, but turns away again, grabbing the back of his neck.

"I'm sorry, George."

At Judy's comment, George whips around to face her. "No. *I'm* sorry. You don't know how sorry I am." George pulls up short, takes a deep breath, smiles and chuckles. "You're joking. Right?"

"I wish I were," Judy says apologetically.

George turns aways from her again and punches the palm of one hand with a fist from the other. Then he bites down on his fist.

"I am so, so sorry," Judy whines.

George snaps his fingers, appearing to have an epiphany. He turns toward Judy once again as if he has found an answer that will clear everything up.

"You were asleep when I found you in the sanctuary. Maybe you just dreamed you had an abortion."

"I don't know how much of tonight I dreamed," Judy admits. "But I *did* have an abortion. That is a medical fact."

"Are you telling me Becca had a sister or a brother and never knew it?" George interrogates. "Or does Becca know and I'm the only one in the dark?"

"Becca has no idea."

"Good," George bellows. "I wish *I* didn't. I can't believe you kept this from me."

"I am sorry, George," Judy says as if pleading for George to calm down.

"Is that all you can say, 'I'm sorry, George'?" He rants on, now quite unhinged. "This is bigger than you, and an apology won't make it go away. You're not only talking about keeping a horrible, hideous, horrendous secret from your husband. You just admitted to killing your child – *my* child." George motions between them with both of his hands as if to complete the picture. "*Our child.*" George escalates, pounding his fist on his chest. "Without so much as consulting me!"

Judy jumps up and holds her hand in front of George defensively to stop his tirade. "I didn't kill our child."

"Isn't that what abortion means?" George says without missing a beat. "Killing an unborn baby?" Judy slowly walks around the arm of the sofa on her end and poises herself facing George.

"You were not the father, George," Judy confesses, expecting the worst.

George looks stunned and stares at Judy in amazement for a moment before sinking back down onto his spot on the sofa. He buries his face in his hands. "If there was ever a time to take the Lord's name in vain..."

"Please don't do that, George," Judy pleads. "Not here, not now, not ever. Curse me. Not God."

George sits up straight. "Oh, that makes me feel all better," he says mockingly before turning deathly serious. "If it wasn't my child, then whose...?"

"Does it really matter?"

George leaps to his feet causing Judy to step back. "You better believe it matters," George bellows again. "I just got hit with a left-right combination to the jaw. *Oh, I had an abortion*," he mimics her with greatly exaggerated intonation in his voice. "Pow!" He swings his left fist in the air. "Oh, *and you're not the father*. Pow again!" George punches the air with his right fist. "I'm punch drunk. My knees are wobbly. The third punch might put me on the canvas for the count." George turns toward Judy and takes a step. "But why not? Let me have it. Do I know him?"

Judy ponders for a moment. Not to determine whether or not she knows the answer, but to determine if she should supply it.

"No. You never met him."

"Does he know who I am?" George fumes.

Judy ponders for another moment. "No," she says, shaking her head.

"Did this happen after we were married?"

"No."

"While we were engaged?"

Judy looks toward George for a moment as if to say she is tiring of the questions. But she sighs instead, accepting that her husband has a right to know. "The abortion took place while we were engaged," she explains. "The conception took place before you and I slept together."

George turns away from Judy again and takes a few steps before stopping. He brushes his raincoat back and holds his hands on his hips. "You kept this from me for the entire length of our marriage," he says with amazement. "I thought I knew you, Judy. I thought I could trust you."

"George, are you telling me that you were never with another woman before we got engaged?" Judy dares to say.

George keeps his posture as he ponders Judy's question for a beat. "Touché," he concedes. He turns, walks back to the sofa, and sits down again at his end. He rests one arm on the back of the sofa and the other on the arm of the sofa he is leaning on. "Tell me what happened."

"Are you sure you want to know?" Judy cautions.

"Are you ashamed to tell me?"

"I don't know if I would call it shame exactly," Judy qualifies.

"We must have been dating at the time," George reasons. "We would have known by then we were going to get engaged."

Judy walks back around the arm of the sofa that was between her and George and sits against it. "He was an old boyfriend from junior high and high school," she begins. "But he wasn't the type of boy my parents would have approved of. When I went off to college where I met you, he joined the Army." She pauses for a moment to see how George is taking her news.

George makes a circular motion in the air, encouraging her to continue.

"He was home on leave just before being deployed to the Middle East," Judy goes on. "That's when I ran into him."

"Did you ever see him again?"

"No." Judy's answer makes it sound as if she hopes it will end the inquiry.

"Did he ever know you got pregnant?"

"Yes," Judy answers, resigned to finish the conversation her confession began.

"Did you consider marrying him instead of me?"

"When I wrote and told him," Judy responds, hoping she can distract George from the romance question, "he wrote back and told me the baby was my problem and, if I didn't want it, to go get rid of it." Judy pauses and looks toward the ceiling. "That's what he actually wrote," she recalls, fighting back tears from the old days. "Quote: 'Get rid of it,' unquote. I was in such shock from being pregnant and then from the way he treated me – I denied the whole thing and pretended it didn't happen. I accepted your proposal, praying that a miracle would happen and my period would start again. But it didn't."

George shakes his head in amazement. "Unbelievable."

"I didn't know what to do, George. I didn't want anyone to find out. So, I called the abortion facility like they taught us in junior high school." Judy reflects for a moment. "The night after the procedure was the first good night's sleep I'd had for months." She pauses before continuing. "And the last good night's sleep I've had since."

"Why didn't you come to church and talk to somebody here?" George asks, suddenly trying to rescue his wife.

"I was afraid to bring my problem to the church. I didn't want to be judged or shamed by some pious parishioner. If there had been someone to talk to about my pregnancy without being condemned, I might not have aborted my baby. I hoped the pain and the shame would eventually subside, but they just became worse and worse with each passing year. I eventually met with Phil alone after you and I stopped coming to see him together and told him my story."

George's countenance visibly softens. "That doesn't say much for us Christians, does it?" he says. "So, Phil has known for a while?"

"I made him promise not to tell you," Judy confesses. "But sharing this with him didn't lessen the pain." Judy and George exchange a long glance.

"Where is the father now?"

"Right before I called the abortion facility, I heard he had been killed in a missile strike," Judy reminisces. "That's what finally pushed me through the abortion facility door."

"The father never knew that you 'got rid of it'?"

Judy shakes her head back and forth.

George goes deeper. "Did you love him?"

"I don't know," Judy responds. "But it hurt me more when he rejected our baby than it did when I heard he had died."

"What was the baby's name?" George asks tenderly, seeing Judy is emotionally wounded.

"I never gave her one."

Puzzlement returns to George's face. "That's what you said about the counselor."

"I didn't even know my first child was a girl until tonight."

"Did the counselor tell you that?" George asks suspiciously.

Judy looks directly into George's eyes. "The counselor *was* my first child."

There is a long pause as George tries to piece things together. "You don't mean the counselor was the one you aborted?" Judy nods enthusiastically now that her secret has found its way into the light. Her lips curl into a smile.

George stands up and walks around the arm of the sofa he has been leaning against and stares at Judy. After a long moment he starts to smile and eventually laughs even harder than he had when he first accused Judy of joking. "Oh, brother. You are too much. You had me going until just then. You can't mean the counselor woman you talked to tonight was your child?"

Judy stands and faces George. "I believe it with all my heart."

"Oh, come *on*, Judy. Did the counselor tell you that? Did she plant that notion in your head? Now I can see why this whole thing seems so surreal. Because it's *not* real. You dreamed the whole thing."

"I can't tell if my conversation with my first daughter tonight was real or not," Judy pleads, anxious for George to believe her. "But that doesn't change the truth of Christ's love. The message she brought to me was the truth Jesus wanted me to know. That's what matters most. I believe the message she brought to me came from God Himself." Judy points heavenward. "I could see it in her eyes."

George dismisses Judy's explanation. "I was buying into the soldier, the pregnancy, the abortion, the whole thing," George chuckles in relief, "hook, line, and sinker. Okay, I believe everything up to the counselor being your daughter."

Judy just looks at George and sighs.

George looks at Judy as he collapses into his spot on the sofa, relieved.

"George, I know you are in shock. I'm in shock," Judy acknowledges.

George waves his hand back and forth. "Give it up, Judy. Enough is enough."

"Do you think this is any less traumatic for me than it is for you?" Judy adds emphatically.

"Color me PTSD," George plays along. "And super-size the T." George makes a time-out signal with his hands.

"George, my abortion left a wound that time won't heal," Judy shares. "Dream or no dream, I believe with all my heart that God used my first daughter to convince me that He loves me in spite of what I did to her and to assure me that He is taking care of her. Can you believe that thirty years of regret, guilt, sorrow, and shame are gone? Poof. I've never believed more in the presence and power of the Holy Spirit than I believe right now."

"The Holy Spirit is not something we talk much about in this church. I'll give you that," George admits.

"George, you have every right to hate me. I know that. To hate me forever."

There is a long pause as George decides what to do with Judy's comment. He sighs, stands up, and walks to the bookcase as Judy waits and watches in silence. After a moment, George turns and looks back at her. "Hate is not what I'm feeling right now." There is a calmness in George's voice. "Much to my surprise, it's not. It's something else."

"What is it?" Judy takes her turn to pry – apparently as surprised as George by his muted reaction.

"I sense God telling me to climb down from my judgment seat and let this all go," he answers. "Everything I think I should be saying, I suddenly don't feel like saying. Everything I feel I should be thinking, I'm not thinking."

Judy walks around the arm of the sofa and sits again. "What *are* you thinking?"

"Regardless of what happened to you, God brought me here tonight – twice – to teach me something. What you said about me and other women before we got engaged is true. But my behavior is too easily buried under the whole abortion thing. There was never an abortion without a man involved. Nothing you said about yourself tonight is not true of me."

"You didn't have an abortion, George. I did."

George walks from the bookcase to the back of the sofa. "It doesn't matter." George is the one pleading now. "Had you come to me with this dilemma back in the day, if I had been the father, I would have wanted you to abort the baby. I would have driven you to the abortion facility and paid for it."

"I'm still the one who did it," Judy insists.

"This is silly," George exclaims as he walks around his end of the sofa and sits. "It feels like we're arguing over who's the bigger sinner."

Judy breathes deeply, stands, and strolls behind the sofa. She stops and looks back toward the doorway to the room. She then glances at the handkerchief in her hand.

George begins to tear up. "Judy, I am every bit as sorry as you are."

Judy glances again at the doorway and then at the handkerchief before she bends over and hugs George around the neck from behind.

"And every bit as forgiven," she assures him.

George fights back tears as he reaches up and strokes Judy's arms.

"What happens now?" George asks tearfully. "What happens to *us* now? Is there even an us anymore?"

Judy continues around the sofa and sits again, this time closer to George. She offers him the handkerchief.

"Thanks," he mutters, accepting it.

"No worries," Judy assures him. "I was afraid you were going to start blowing your nose on your sleeve."

George wipes his tears with the handkerchief and then holds the handkerchief up to his nose as if to blow.

Judy snatches it out of his hand before he can. "Don't you dare! Use your sleeve!"

"What?" George exclaims.

"I told you this is mine forever," Judy insists.

George looks puzzled for a moment, then curious.

"Did the counselor touch that?"

"She wiped my tears with it, and I wiped hers," Judy says sentimentally.

George stares at the handkerchief in Judy's hand. "May I," he asks sheepishly, "may I hold it again?"

Judy begins to hand it to George cautiously, but suddenly snatches it back.

"No blowing," she commands.

"You don't have to let me hold it."

"Oh, shut up, you goof. You can hold it as long as you remember it's mine forever."

"I cross my heart and hope to die," he promises before catching himself ignoring the fact that death is central to their whole conversation. "Sorry."

Judy hands the handkerchief to George who accepts it delicately as if not to break it. He looks down at the handkerchief, then back at Judy, and smiles. Judy smiles back. George gently folds the handkerchief over and over several times into an increasingly smaller triangle. He then hands it back to Judy with two hands as a funeral color guard might present a folded flag to a widow. Judy accepts it with both hands.

George suddenly grasps her hands in his as he scoots closer to her on the sofa. "Please say there is still an us," he begs.

"We are more an us in this moment than we've ever been," Judy assures her husband. "And we're grandparents," she adds with hopeful anticipation in her voice.

"We have a pregnant daughter who may or may not keep her baby," George mitigates.

"Regardless," she insists, "we have a grandchild at this moment. "We're not dreaming that."

"Do you know how Becca feels about it?"

"Becca is very clear that it's her choice."

"On a practical level, it is her choice," George reasons. "We can't stop her if she's determined to terminate her pregnancy."

"No more than anyone could have stopped me," Judy agrees. "But, without knowing the whole truth," Judy holds up one hand, palm facing up, "versus the lie," she holds up the other hand, palm up, "women don't have a real choice. Only a lie."

"Becca went to church and Sunday School as a child…" George protests. "…Where she was never taught about the sanctity of life," Judy completes his sentence.

"Are you going to tell Becca about her sister?" George asks.

"As Becca's mother, the most honest thing I can do is to let her know that she *has* a sister. And then, let her do with that information what she will. At least she will know the truth and never feel the need to say, *Mom, if I had only known what this would be like, I would have never done it.*"

George ponders for a moment before speaking. "Becca is pregnant with *our* grandchild. Let's talk to her *together.*"

"That sounds like a great 'choice' to me," Judy smiles.

George takes her hands in his again. "And *our* choice?" he asks. "What are we going to decide about us?"

Judy releases one hand and playfully coaxes George closer with her index finger.

George scoots closer to her.

"I'm sorry for many of the choices I've made in my life," she begins, "especially my abortion." Judy reaches out her finger again, this time tickling George under the chin. "But I'm not the least bit sorry for choosing you." She smiles, joining both of their hands again.

An astonished George shakes his head side to side. "Who *are* you? And what have you done with my wife?"

"I'm a free woman," Judy laughs as if just being released from death row. "Free beyond any kind of freedom I've ever imagined. You are not acting like the George I've come to know for over thirty years either."

"This is a dream come true," George grins. "I'm feeling younger by the minute." He pulls one hand out of Judy's and strokes his head.

"I can even feel color coming back into my hair." George returns his hand to Judy's grasp.

Judy giggles and smiles as she looks down at George's watch. "George, look!"

"Look at what?"

"Look at the time," she blurts, holding his hand up to show him his own watch.

George glances at his watch and then pulls his hand away from Judy and examines it more closely. "It's six o'clock. Straight up," he exclaims. He taps on his watch several times. "My watch must have stopped."

Judy looks at her watch.

"Mine, too?" She taps on her watch several times. "This is no co-incidence."

"Is that the time you went to the…?" George's voice trails off.

Judy nods her head as her cell phone starts playing, "Isn't she lovely?" by Stevie Wonder.

"It's Becca," she recognizes as she dives for the phone in her purse. Pulling it out, Judy presses the screen to answer. "Hi, Sweetie. What's up?"

George slides closer to Judy to listen in and motions for her to put the call on speaker. Judy presses her screen again.

"Are you guys at home?" Becca's voice comes over the speaker, crying.

"No, your dad and I are at the church. What's wrong, honey?"

"I really need to talk to you guys. When will you be home?"

"In ten minutes," George pipes in. "Are you okay?"

"Something really amazing just happened and I need to talk to you," Becca answers. "I'll meet you at your house."

Becca hangs up.

"Becca…?" Judy calls into the phone. She turns to George. "She hung up. You don't think…"

"Our daughter needs us," George declares as he stands and heads to the door to grab Judy's raincoat. Judy grabs her purse and follows him. "That's all I need to know." He helps Judy on with her coat. Judy and George start out the door. Just as George reaches for the light switch, Judy stops him and turns, suddenly serene.

"Hey," she says. George stops. "There's one more thing I need to confess."

"Do I need to 'settle' again?" George asks suspiciously with a glance back toward the wing chair.

Judy grabs George by the tie, pulls his face close to hers, and kisses him passionately on the lips. "I love you," she croons before releasing George's tie and heading out into the hall, flipping off the light switch as she exits.

George, frozen in place, raises his hand toward his lips and smiles.

"Come on now," Judy calls back to him. "Our daughter needs us. Remember?"

George comes back into the moment and joins her scampering down the short flight of steps to the big wooden doors in the light of the red EXIT sign. He pushes one door open to let her out as his wife retrieves her car keys. The rain is still pouring outside. Judy flips her raincoat hood over her head and presses on her key fob to unlock her car. Despite her hood, George raises his coat high with both his hands to shield her from the rain as they scamper to her car. He opens her driver's side door, and she hops in, starting the engine as he closes the door behind her.

"Hurry now," she says again as she rolls down her window and motions him toward his car. She rolls her window up against the rain and backs out of her parking place.

George watches her go for a moment before reaching into his coat pocket and unlocking his car, which is in the next parking spot. He begins to climb in but hesitates, looks back at the wooden entry doors to the church. He closes his car door, runs over, and tugs on the door handle expecting it to still be unlocked. It won't open. Finding it locked for the first time that evening, George stands in the rain for a moment, tries the door one more time, and finds it still locked. He backs away from the entry doors slowly, then turns, unlocks his car door again, and begins to climb in, pausing for an instant to look at the wooden entry doors one last time before climbing in and starting his car.

From the basement nursery window, the brake lights and turn signal on George's car are visible as he pulls onto the street. All that remains visible are raindrops running down the glass.

SUPPORT AFTER ABORTION CONTACT INFORMATION

***Viable* and the online post-abortion healing journey**

If you feel emotionally impacted after finishing this book and/or the online Healing Journey, *Viable Act II*, you can reach out to Support After Abortion to receive post-abortive counseling and, if you want, a referral to more intensive and comprehensive post-abortion healing programs. Here's how:

Call or text 844-289-4673

or

Write to Help@SupportAfterAbortion.com

If you feel an immediate and urgent need to discuss your pregnancy or abortion-related issue with a live Christian coach after office hours. or on weekends and holidays, call H3Helpline 24/7 at 866-721-7881.

To watch a free video recording of the full one-act play, *Viable: The Truth of Christ's Love,* and/or see a preview of *Viable Act II*, visit *ViablePlay.org.*

KAREN DESCRIBES HOW *VIABLE* CAME TO THE STAGE

I was crossing the square at St. James Church in Medjugorje, Bosnia-Herzegovina, when he called out to me. Although I had never met him, the Nigerian priest, who had traveled with our group of pilgrims from New York City, was one of many priests from across the globe, hearing confessions from the quilt of humanity queuing up prior to attending evening Communion Mass.

"I have a message for you!" he exclaimed.

"From whom?" I asked.

With calm conviction, he said, "From God."

"Oh!" was my stunned response. He went on to tell me that I was to become active in the pro-life movement.

Ever since experiencing a late-term miscarriage, my heart has been pro-life. But I had never engaged in activism. Now, with the Nigerian priest's words, my life was about to change in ways I never anticipated.

Arriving back in the United States, a longtime friend, John Hill, met me at Atlanta's Hartsfield airport to drive me to my South Carolina home. He was excited to hear about the trip as well as the progress of a book I was writing.

"Karen, would you mind if I give your phone number to John Hoover? He is also a writer and lives in New York City. You two have a great deal in common."

Because I lived part-time in NYC, meeting John would be a pleasure. He had already published over a dozen books, and my circle of friends included other prolific authors.

Several days after I arrived home, John called. Our conversation was wonderfully easy, almost as if we had known one another for years. After exchanging bios, John told me he had written a new play and would appreciate another pair of creative eyes to read it. "What's it about?" I asked.

"It's a pro-life play called *Viable.*"

I gasped. My heart began to pound, and the chair in which I sat rolled back from my desk. John sent the script, which was only 102 double-spaced pages long. Nevertheless, it took me nearly three weeks to complete reading it because I had to keep putting it down to wipe away tears and regroup.

Why? *Viable* was no mere pro-life message redux, it was heavenly trumpets for life, not just for the unborn, but for the viability of humanity. The words I read, which John credits to the Holy Spirit, created one of the most profound modern-day Christian messages of forgiveness, redemption, and restoration I had ever read. Even though I wept reading the script, tears still fill my eyes knowing how three strangers had been chosen to be part of God's almighty will. The Holy Spirit that inspired these words had placed a pilgrim, a priest, and a playwright into His plan. How all of this would unfold is a miracle that required time to embrace. John and I plotted a pathway to get *Viable* on the stage.

South Carolina Citizens for Life (SCCL) holds its annual fundraising dinner in January, just prior to the opening of the legislative session. I met the women responsible for the organization when I attended for the first time in January 2019. They were short of funds for the dinner event. On a God-wink impulse, I wrote a check to cover the shortfall. What had not yet occurred to me was His might at work— He was systematically placing passionate pro-life people together. All would soon begin manifesting with glory!

After workshopping the play in the months that followed, *Viable's* first public performance premiered in the chapel of First Presbyterian Church in Greenville, SC, in June 2019. I had no idea that the President of SCCL was a longtime member of that church. The performance stunned the overflow audience. There was a reason each pew had packs of tissues. Behind the actors, a cross loomed large, light radiating from it. The Holy Spirit was among us, filling the chapel with His love. Women wept as men wiped away tears of their own. Christ lived among us and pulled *Viable* forward. In January

2020, after several more performances, including a university and the National Right to Life annual conference, *Viable* was performed to the largest attendance and single night of giving in SCCL's Proudly Pro-Life Dinner history.

The power of one for good is the power of God. John Hoover was chosen to bring Christ's message of redemption to women and men who "know not what they do" when they opt to abort their children because of false political narratives. "So it is not the will of your Father who is in Heaven that one of the little ones perish" (Matthew 18:14 ESV). *Viable* is not a judgment—it is a one act play of the Lord's promises of mercy and salvation, which has, since 2020, been performed over 40 times in 12 states, covering more than 40,000 miles of touring. Now it is a small book as well as still touring the country on stage.

SCCL has struggled for 50 years to pass pro-life legislation. Far too many legislators and constituents fail to grasp the cumulative impacts abortion has heaped upon men and women manipulated to believe in political chicanery, upon forgotten fathers, broken families, and a broken culture. In 2023, SCCL passed the Heartbeat Bill in South Carolina. It took 49 years to do it. What made the difference? Awakening. In Spring of 2024, the defeat of three pro-choice Republican female state senators sent shock waves across the state and hope to other pro-life organizations. SCCL is now one of the most powerful pro-life nonprofits in the United States. How did we achieve this? Isaiah 60:1: "Arise, shine, for your light has come, and the glory of the Lord rises upon you" (NIV).

Songwriters Chris Wallin and Rachel Holt (Baste Records) collaborated to write, produce, and perform "I Was Going to be a Girl," which causes tears to flow from my eyes as often as I listen to it. Here are the final 46 words...

Yeah, I was gonna change the world.
I was gonna be a girl.
The first thing I was gonna do
Was breathe and fall in love with you.
But a couple of weeks before I saw the light,
Mine flickered out when you changed your mind.

A pilgrim, a priest, and a playwright have a message for you.

From whom?

God.

To my dear friend, John Hoover, you are doing the Lord's work and have forever changed the lives of thousands with the magnificent production of *Viable*. My life has been enriched by your vision to show the humility, grace, peace, and joy of Christ's promise to all who seek salvation. May God bless you and *Viable*—the book of renewal. With a grateful heart...

Karen Iacovelli Forster, Board Member
South Carolina Citizens For Life
October 2025

ABOUT THE SCRIBE

To the man who typed the words on these pages, it seemed like God was dictating this book and the play it is based upon, *ViablePlay.org*. John Hoover was deeply impacted while attending a sanctity of life lecture in 1982 at First Evangelical Free Church in Fullerton, California, where he became active while writing and producing for the Entertainment Division at Disneyland.

When the time came, John followed God's leading and wrote what had been placed on his heart 36 years earlier. By then, John was a seasoned, multi-published writer of over a dozen commercially-published books who was quite aware of when the words he was writing originated with him or from an intelligence greater than his own. The play and book, *Viable*, were like taking dictation from a higher authority. He credits the Holy Spirit, not himself, as the author and playwright.

John holds master's degrees in Marriage and Family Therapy, Human and Organization Development, and a PhD in Human and Organizational Systems. In addition to writing books (many on bestseller lists including one on the New York Times bestseller list) for American Management Association/HarperCollins Leadership, Barnes & Noble

Publishing, Inc, Career Press, McGraw-Hill, St. Martin's Press, Sage, and Wiley (some published in 24 languages), John writes, produces, and directs corporate stage and film projects, educational films, and television pilots. He lectures on leadership and media psychology, is an International Coach Federation Master Certified Life and Leadership Coach, is a Presidential member of the American Association of Christian Counselors, provides pro-bono Christian mentoring for men emerging from drug and alcohol addiction, chairs church committees, and works to defend the sanctity of life from conception to natural death.